STARK LIBRARY

Dinosaurs

Styracosaurus

by Julie Murray

Dash!
LEVELED READERS
An Imprint of Abdo Zoom • abdobooks.com

Dash!
LEVELED READERS

Level 1 – Beginning
Short and simple sentences with familiar words or patterns for children who are beginning to understand how letters and sounds go together.

Level 2 – Emerging
Longer words and sentences with more complex language patterns for readers who are practicing common words and letter sounds.

Level 3 – Transitional
More developed language and vocabulary for readers who are becoming more independent.

THIS BOOK CONTAINS RECYCLED MATERIALS

abdobooks.com

Published by Abdo Zoom, a division of ABDO, PO Box 398166, Minneapolis, Minnesota 55439. Copyright © 2023 by Abdo Consulting Group, Inc. International copyrights reserved in all countries. No part of this book may be reproduced in any form without written permission from the publisher. Dash!™ is a trademark and logo of Abdo Zoom.

Printed in the United States of America, North Mankato, Minnesota.
052022
092022

Photo Credits: Alamy, Getty Images, Science Source, Shutterstock
Production Contributors: Kenny Abdo, Jennie Forsberg, Grace Hansen, John Hansen
Design Contributors: Candice Keimig, Neil Klinepier

Library of Congress Control Number: 2021950312

Publisher's Cataloging in Publication Data
Names: Murray, Julie, author.
Title: Styracosaurus / by Julie Murray
Description: Minneapolis, Minnesota : Abdo Zoom, 2023 | Series: Dinosaurs | Includes online resources and index.
Identifiers: ISBN 9781098228309 (lib. bdg.) | ISBN 9781098229146 (ebook) | ISBN 9781098229566 (Read-to-Me ebook)
Subjects: LCSH: Styracosaurus--Juvenile literature. | Dinosaurs--Juvenile literature. | Paleontology--Juvenile literature. | Extinct animals--Juvenile literature.
Classification: DDC 567.90--dc23

Table of Contents

Styracosaurus 4

More Facts 22

Glossary 23

Index 24

Online Resources 24

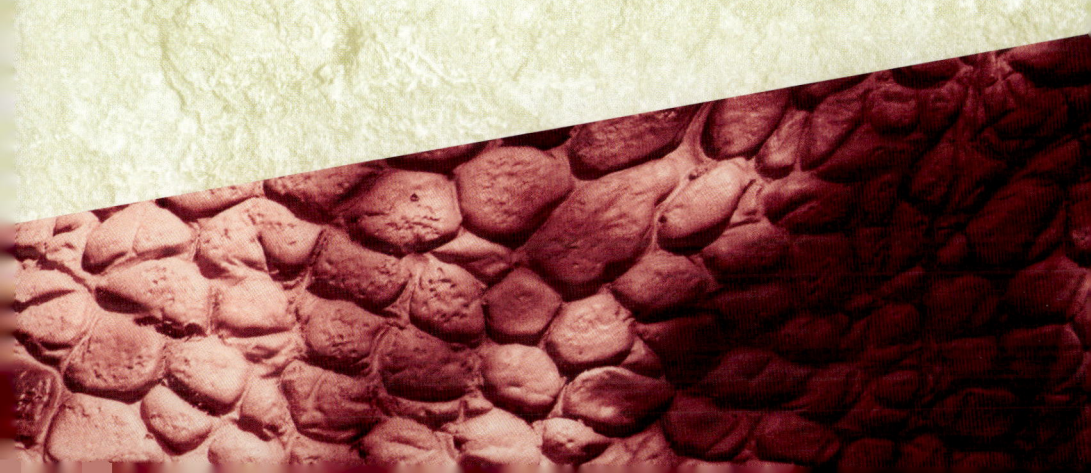

Styracosaurus

Styracosaurus was a **ceratopsian** dinosaur. It lived 75 million years ago.

5

It was 18 feet (5.5 m) long. It weighed 6,000 pounds (2,721 kg).

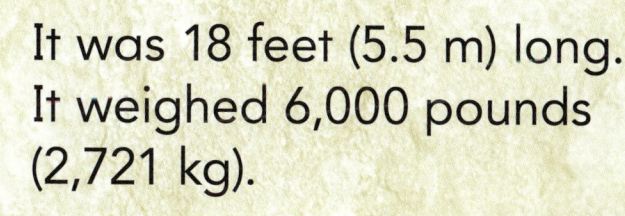

It had four short legs. Its body was thick and strong.

It had a **frill** on the back of its head. Four to six spikes grew out of the frill.

Styracosaurus had a long horn on its nose. The horn was nearly 2 feet (0.6 m) long.

12

The **frill** and horn were used to scare away **predators** and to fight.

14

15

16

Styracosaurus had a small beak. Its beak was good at tearing apart plants.

It only ate plants. It liked to eat ferns and palms.

The first **fossils** were discovered in Alberta, Canada, by Charles M. Sternberg. The dinosaur was named in 1913.

More Facts

- *Styracosaurus* means "spiked lizard."

- It could run up to 20 mph (32 kph).

- It lived in a group. This gave it protection.

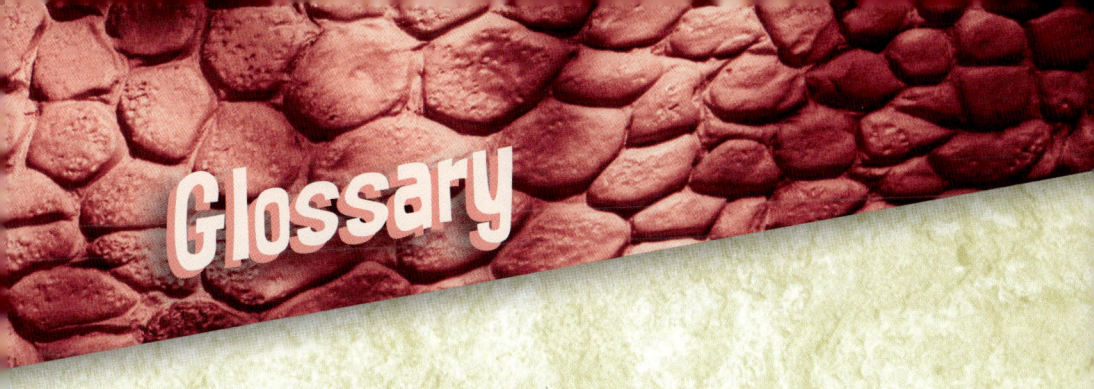

Glossary

ceratopsian – a plant-eating dinosaur of a group whose members are typically four-legged, solidly built, and have enormous skulls, sharp beaks, and long horns.

fossil – the remains or trace of a living animal or plant from a long time ago. Fossils are found embedded in earth or rock.

frill – a projection of bone from the neck of an animal.

predator – an animal that hunts other animals for food.

Index

Alberta, Canada 20

beak 17

body 8

ceratopsian 4

food 17, 19

fossils 20

frill 11, 14

head 11

horn 12, 14

legs 8

protection 14

size 7

Sternberg, Charles M. 20

weight 7

Online Resources

Booklinks
NONFICTION NETWORK
FREE! ONLINE NONFICTION RESOURCES

To learn more about Styracosaurus, please visit **abdobooklinks.com** or scan this QR code. These links are routinely monitored and updated to provide the most current information available.